MINISTERS OF HOLY COMMUNION

A Practical and Liturgical Guide

Donald A. Withey

Member of the Committee for Pastoral Liturgy
Bishops' Conference of England & Wales

Decani Books

Decani Books

First published in 1990 by the St Thomas More Centre, Hendon.
This edition published in 1997 by Decani Books, 30 North Terrace, Mildenhall,
Suffolk IP28 7AB

© 1990 Donald A.Withey

Frontispiece: Calligram by Claire Smith

Printed by RPM Reprographics (Chichester) Ltd, Units 2-3 Spur Road, Quarry Lane,
Chichester, West Sussex, P019 2PR

to

my daughter Anne

The
Lord Jesus,
on the same night
in which he was betrayed,
took bread; and when he had
⟶ GIVEN THANKS ⟶
he broke it and said: "Take eat;
this is My Body which is
broken for you; do this
in remembrance
of me."

In the same manner he also took
the cup after supper, saying:"This cup
is the New Covenant in my blood.
This do, as often as you drink it,
in remembrance of me."⟶
For as often as you
eat this
bread
and
drink this cup
you
proclaim
the Lord's death
till he comes.⟶I COR.II:23-26

Calligram by Claire Smith

Acknowledgements

I would like to express my sincere thanks to Father Pat O'Donovan of the Diocese of Clifton, who made it all possible; to Stephen Dean for his kindness in publishing both editions of this book; to my daughter Claire Smith for the calligram which forms the frontispiece; to Norman Paton for the photographs, and to Pam, my wife, in appreciation of her invaluable help and encouragement in the writing of this book.

CONTENTS

CONTENTS

Introduction

HAVE YOU BEEN INVITED BY YOUR PARISH PRIEST to become a Minister of Holy Communion? Perhaps you felt hesitant about accepting when the priest first asked you.

This book has been written to help you to prepare for this ministry. It is complete in itself and covers in detail both the practical skills and the background knowledge which you will need.

Most ministers feel much more confident when they have had some training and preparation. This can be a happy and enriching experience, and by the time you are officially commissioned by the bishop you will certainly feel ready to carry out this important ministry.

This book is based on courses which have been presented in various parishes. The ministers who attended these courses were kind enough to say that they found them enjoyable and helpful. I hope that you will find the guidance in this book equally helpful.

Please read both parts of this book. The background studies are as important as the practical skills for effective ministry.

CHAPTER ONE

Your Ministry

WHEN YOU HAVE COMPLETED YOUR TRAINING AND PREPARATION, you will be commissioned by the bishop, or his delegate, at a short ceremony which usually takes place at Mass and in the presence of the people of the parish whom you are going to serve.

'Ministry' means 'service', service to God and to your fellow Christians. The keynote of Christian ministry is love, and during the Rite of Commissioning the bishop reminds the ministers of the words of Our Lord:

> I give you a new commandment:
> love one another;
> just as I have loved you,
> you also must love one another.
> By this love you have for one another,
> everyone will know that you are my disciples.
>
> *John 13:34-35*

St. Paul reminds us (Ephesians 4:1-13) of the diversity of ministries in the Church and of their importance. The Church's liturgy is celebrated by the whole people of God. The conduct of the liturgy, especially the Mass, entails particular responsibilities not only for the ordained ministers (bishops, priests and deacons) but also for non-ordained lay ministers (ministers of holy communion, servers, readers, commentators, ushers, collectors, musicians, singers, animators, sacristans and others).

The 'ordinary' ministers of holy communion are bishops, priests and deacons: they distribute holy communion by right of their ordination. The lay ministers are, technically speaking, 'extraordinary' ministers of the eucharist because they do not exercise their functions by virtue of possessing orders. But the title 'extraordinary minister' is liable to be misunderstood, so it is less used now. Even the expression 'special minister' is now less common. Most people prefer the simple and natural title of 'minister of holy communion'.

The office of minister of holy communion is not to be seen as a temporary makeshift arrangement. It is not a novelty invented by certain enthusiasts. It is an official ministry set up with full authority by the Church, and included in the Code of Canon Law (see note at the end of this chapter). It has a dignity and function of its own, and ministers are individually authorised and commissioned by the bishop of the diocese.

It is important for ministers to understand that the office of minister of holy communion was officially instituted by Pope Paul VI in 1973. Faculties to appoint these ministers were granted to bishops in the Instruction of the Congregation for the Discipline of the Sacraments (as it was then called) entitled *Immensae Caritatis* issued on 20 January 1973. This Instruction is well worth reading. In it the Holy See made it clear why the ministry had been instituted by the Pope. The guiding principle is the spiritual good of the faithful. Reception of holy communion must not become impossible or difficult because of a shortage of priests or because a priest is not available.

With the reforms of the Second Vatican Council, the relaxation of the fasting rules, and a growing understanding of the significance of the Mass and of the sacrament of the Holy Eucharist, a much larger proportion of our congregations is receiving communion at every Mass. Most parishes now have fewer clergy, many only one priest. Congregations at Mass on Sundays and Days of Obligation are often large. This alone will justify the use of ministers. The need for them is even greater now that we have permission in England and Wales to have communion under both kinds.

The increase in the reception of holy communion and the permission to receive the chalice are developments for which we must give thanks to God. In this context, the institution of ministers of holy communion is very welcome. Ministers exercise a noble office, confident in the knowledge that by their ministry they are serving their fellow-Catholics and promoting their spiritual well-being by making it possible for Christ's body and blood to be received by the faithful.

Your preparation for this ministry falls into three parts:

1. Spiritual formation

Ministers should be committed to deepening and enriching their own spiritual lives. Their work as ministers should be approached through prayer, reflection and the reading of the scriptures.

2. Instruction

Ministers should have some understanding of the idea of ministry, the Mass, the sacrament of the Holy Eucharist, and of communion under both kinds. The chapters in Part Two of this book are designed to help you cover this groundwork.

3. Skill Training

The chapters in the first part of this book are designed to help you acquire the essential skills which you will need as a minister. These skills are presented in considerable detail because experience has shown that most ministers welcome detailed guidance. It is important for ministers to be trained in all aspects of their ministry as they are now authorised to carry out a number of duties when a priest is not available.

CANON LAW

Ministers of Holy Communion now have authority to carry out their duties in accordance with the provisions of canon law.

The following sections of the new Code of Canon Law, issued by Pope John Paul II in 1983, are relevant to ministers:

230.3   Where the needs of the Church require and ministers are not available, lay people... can supply certain of their functions, that is, exercise the ministry of the word, preside over liturgical prayers, confer baptism and distribute holy communion...

910.1   The ordinary minister of holy communion is a bishop, a priest or a deacon.

910.2   The extraordinary minister of holy communion is an acolyte, or another of Christ's faithful deputed to act in accordance with canon 230.3.

911.1   The duty and right to bring the blessed Eucharist to the sick as Viaticum belongs to the parish priest, to assistant priests... (etc.)

911.2   In a case of necessity, or with the permission at least presumed of the parish priest, chaplain or superior, who must subsequently be notified, any priest or other minister of holy communion must do this.

943   The minister of exposition of the blessed Sacrament and of the eucharistic blessing is a priest or deacon. In special circumstances the minister of exposition and deposition alone, but without the blessing, is an acolyte, an extraordinary minister of holy communion, or another person deputed by the local Ordinary, in accordance with the regulations of the diocesan bishop.

PART ONE

SKILL TRAINING

CHAPTER TWO

General Routines for Ministers

WE BEGIN OUR PRACTICAL SKILL TRAINING by considering the general routines to be followed by ministers at Mass. To avoid overloading this chapter, the actual distribution of hosts and the administration of the chalice will be dealt with separately in the next two chapters.

Experience shows that ministers much prefer to have a series of clear and simple routines to follow as they then feel more confident and assured. The suggestions which follow are offered simply as possible guidelines. It is for each parish to work out an order which is the most suitable for its own circumstances.

(I would like to ask my readers please to understand all references throughout this book to ministers or members of the congregation to apply equally to both sexes, even if sometimes, to avoid a cumbersome style, I refer simply to 'him' or 'his.')

The number of ministers

If the congregation is small, it will be sufficient for the priest to distribute the hosts and two ministers to administer chalices. For a large congregation, the priest will need to be assisted by a 'hosts minister' and four 'chalice ministers'. If the congregation is very large, or if movement around the church is difficult because of space restrictions, it may be necessary to have some additional distribution points elsewhere in the church: if so, then more ministers will be required. The general rule is to have twice as many chalice ministers as host ministers because it takes longer to administer the chalice than to give someone a host. The most suitable number of ministers for a particular church is best decided in the light of experience.

Remember that the celebrant normally distributes hosts. If there is a deacon officiating at Mass, he will administer a chalice. On occasions when additional priests or deacons are present, they should distribute Holy Communion, which means that some or all of the lay ministers will not be required on that occasion. It is forbidden for priests and deacons, who are, of course, the 'ordinary' ministers of Holy Communion, to sit down and leave the distribution to lay ministers.

The distribution of Holy Communion

Let us assume that there are five ministers taking part in the distribution, namely one host minister (=HM), two chalice ministers on the left-hand side of the church (i.e. the congregation's left) (=CL1 and CL2) and two chalice ministers on the right (=CR1 and CR2). At the end of the 'Lamb of God' (not *during* it, as this would distract attention from that important and significant action, the fraction or breaking of the consecrated bread), the ministers come from their places in the congregation, genuflect together on the sanctuary, and stand at the sides of the altar as in diagram 1.

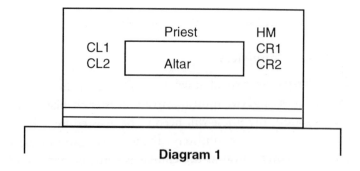

Diagram 1

The ministers remain standing, even though the servers may

kneel down for 'This is the Lamb of God...' If required, HM will go to the tabernacle, take out the ciborium and place it on the altar. However, this should not normally be necessary, as the hosts (arranged in this case in two patens on the altar) should have been consecrated at the same Mass.

After the priest (and other clergy) have received communion, the celebrant will give communion under both kinds to the ministers. The servers then receive hosts from the celebrant and the chalice from one of the chalice ministers.

The ministers are then given their paten or chalice by the priest and they all move to the distribution points. The following diagram assumes that the church is rectangular in shape and shows the ministers' positions accordingly:

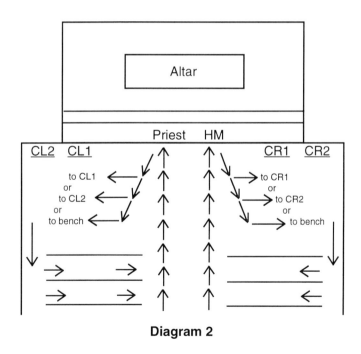

Diagram 2

Notice that the priest and HM are standing on the sanctuary floor for the distribution of hosts, while the chalice ministers are

standing on the nave floor. It is generally better for the host ministers to be standing a little higher than the communicants, and for
the chalice ministers to stand on the same level; but this can be
varied if desired. The chalice ministers are spaced apart as much as
possible to allow room for small queues to form.

The congregation

There should be an orderly system for the congregation to come
up to receive Holy Communion. In a rectangular church with a
centre aisle and two side aisles, as in the diagram, the people can
leave their benches one row at a time, starting with the front row,
and form two queues in the centre aisle. The left-hand queue comes
up to the priest to receive the host. Communicants then move on
to receive the chalice from CL1 or CL2, depending on which 'chalice queue' is the shorter. They then continue down the left aisle
and back to their benches. Communicants not wishing to receive
the chalice simply walk past the chalice ministers and continue
down the side aisle to their seats. Similarly, communicants from
the right-hand benches come up in the right-hand queue, receive
the host from HM, the chalice (if they wish to receive it) from
CR1 or CR2, and then proceed down the right side aisle back to
their seats.

The movement of the congregation needs to be carefully planned
in terms of the shape of the church and the amount of space available. It should be born in mind that no one should feel compelled
in any way to receive the chalice if he or she does not wish to do so;
in which case it should be made possible for the communicant to
receive the host and then walk past the chalices without being made
to feel awkward or conspicuous.

After communion

The priest and the ministers should remain in their distribution positions until all communicants who wish to do so have received the chalice as well as the host. They then proceed as follows.

(a) The host minister returns to the altar with the priest. If there are only one or two hosts left on the paten, they can be consumed by the priest or HM. If there are a considerable number of hosts left, they will need to be placed in the ciborium in the tabernacle. This is done in the following manner. HM should leave his paten on the corporal, go to the tabernacle (see section below on this), open it, take out the ciborium and place it on the corporal on the altar. He removes first the veil and then the lid. Either the priest or HM will put all the unusued hosts into the ciborium. Then HM will replace the lid and the veil and return the ciborium to the tabernacle.

When this has been done, HM takes both patens to the place where the cleansing is to be carried out.

(b) The chalice ministers go to the appropriate place to carry out the cleansing, which is described in the next section. The ministers should consume any consecrated wine left in their chalices. If you feel unable to do this, ask another minister to do it for you; if this is not possible, give the chalice to the priest and he will attend to it. If there is a considerable amount of consecrated wine to be consumed, consume a little at a time. If you are in view of the congregation as you do this, turn your back to the congregation and consume from the chalice in a dignified fashion. This is to avoid criticism which is sometimes made by ill-informed individuals.

The cleansing of the sacred vessels
(also known as the purification or ablutions)

It is highly recommended that this operation should be carried out in a side chapel or in the sacristy, rather than on the sanctuary at the credence table. It is better to carry out the cleansing away from the congregation, especially as this is taking place during the period of silent prayer and reflection following communion and such activity could be distracting.

The chalices are cleansed in the following manner. Any consecrated wine remaining is consumed by the minister. Water is poured into the chalice, either by a server or by the minister. The inside of the chalice is rinsed round with this water, which is then consumed by the minister. The chalice is wiped dry inside and out with the purificator, which should be unfolded for this purpose. Some ministers like to wash their fingers after administering and cleansing the chalice, but there is no rule requiring this to be done. The chalice and purificator are then left in an appropriate place, or handed to the server to take away.

The patens are cleansed in the following manner. Take one of the chalices, brush all crumbs and fragments of host from the paten into the chalice (using the purificator or one's fingers), rinse the chalice round with water, which is then consumed, and wipe the chalice dry with the purificator. Paten, chalice and purificator are then left in an appropriate place, or handed to the server to take away. Ministers must wash their fingers after handling hosts or cleansing a paten. This is in case any crumbs have attached themselves to their fingers.

For the washing of fingers, there will be a bowl, a jug of water and a towel for this purpose. Ministers either wash their fingers themselves, or else a server will be there to pour water over their fingers and offer them the towel.

When the cleansing has been finished, the ministers genuflect together on the sanctuary and return to their seats.

An even better arrangement is for the ministers to take the vessels to the sacristy when the distribution of Holy Communion is finished, consume any consecrated wine left in the chalices, and then leave the vessels there. They return to their places at once and attend to the cleansing after Mass.

The Tabernacle

Ministers need to know the simple procedure for approaching, opening and closing the tabernacle. This should be practised as part of your training. You may have to fetch or replace the ciborium at Mass. You may have to open the tabernacle to obtain hosts to take to the sick. If you are conducting a communion service outside Mass or a service of adoration of the Blessed Sacrament, you will have to open the tabernacle on these occasions also.

Make certain you know where to find the key. During Mass it will usually be next to the tabernacle or on the altar. Go to the tabernacle, open both doors and take out the ciborium. There are no genuflections in front of the tabernacle at this stage. The tabernacle doors are left open. When you are replacing the ciborium, go to the tabernacle, put the vessel inside, close one door, genuflect, close the other door and turn the key. Replace the key in its place. Wash your fingers in the bowl by the tabernacle if you have been handling hosts: you will find a water bowl with a lid and a towel near the tabernacle. If you are immediately going to take part in the cleansing of vessels you can, of course, wash your fingers there instead.

The position of the tabernacle varies greatly in our churches today. Some tabernacles are set at the back of an altar (known as the altar of reservation), others are mounted on a plinth or set in a wall. In the latter case, there is usually only a narrow ledge in front of the tabernacle and it is not advisable to set down the ciborium or to move hosts in such an awkward position, so always take the ciborium to the altar and place it on the corporal. You can then remove the veil, take off the lid, and move hosts without the risk of knocking over the ciborium. On the other hand, if the tabernacle is situated on an altar, there will be room to carry out such operations. An altar of reservation will have its own corporal spread out on which to stand the sacred vessels.

It is important to practise opening the tabernacle doors, especially as some of the older ones are awkwardly designed with stiff locks and hard-to-find keyholes. A tabernacle is not only the place of reservation for the Blessed Sacrament, to which we direct our worship and prayers. It has to be a solid, opaque, unbreakable safe, fixed in some way into the fabric of the building, so that the Sacrament is secured against theft or profanation. Some tabernacles have a veil on the outside, in a liturgical colour. This has to be drawn to one side before the doors are opened. Sometimes there are also little curtains inside the door, and these have to be parted or drawn aside. Many modern tabernacles do not have either of these features.

Perhaps if you have never been near to a tabernacle when it is opened, you may be unsure exactly what is contained inside it. Nowadays, there is often only one vessel, namely a ciborium in which some hosts are reserved, sufficient for sick calls and for those occasions when insufficient hosts have been consecrated at Mass. In busy churches where the priest, regrettably, does not consecrate hosts at each Mass, there will naturally be more hosts reserved and perhaps more than one ciborium.

The norm should be to give the people Holy Communion with hosts consecrated at the same Mass: to use hosts consecrated at a previous Mass is not appropriate, and the Church has repeatedly urged priests not to give communion 'from the tabernacle', most recently in the *General Instruction on the Roman Missal* (56) and in the *Constitution on the Sacred Liturgy* of the Second Vatican Council (55). When a large number of hosts has accumulated in the tabernacle, then of course the priest has to use these at a Mass, preferably alongside some other hosts consecrated at that Mass. Our reception of Holy Communion should be linked to the celebration of the Eucharist in which we are taking part.

Churches which have a regular service of adoration of the Blessed Sacrament (with or without Benediction) keep a special larger host for this purpose. It stands in a lunette and is kept in a pyx designed to hold it. It will be as well to ascertain what is kept in the tabernacle of your church so that you will not be bewildered when you first have to take out a ciborium. The parish priest should familiarise you with this sort of information as part of your training.

Children

If children present themselves for the host and you think they may not have made their first communion, quietly ask the children or the parents about this. Children who have not made their first communion often come up with their parents, and the minister can wish them a blessing by touching their heads and saying 'The blessing of Christ' or something similar.

Children are, of course, at liberty to receive the chalice as a matter of choice from their first communion onwards, and they should be encouraged (and certainly not forbidden) to do so. Arbitrary rules forbidding younger children to receive the host in the hand are also quite unjustified: in countries where permission has been given for reception in the hand, the child has the same right as the adult.

Non-Catholics

Except in certain strictly defined cases, non-Catholics are not permitted to receive Holy Communion in a Catholic Church. The Church may one day permit some degree of inter-communion. At present she does not, taking the view that inter-communion must be the fruit of unity, not an instrument of unity.

In some of our churches, a considerable number of non-Catholics attend Mass, especially in the case of 'inter-faith' marriages. On special occasions also, such as Midnight Mass and Easter, non-Catholics sometimes come to Mass. It is a good plan to invite them to come up with the communicants for a blessing. They indicate that they would like to receive the blessing by crossing their arms across their chest. This practice has been well-received in many churches, and it prevents embarrassment. More importantly, it is a loving gesture to our fellow-Christians with whom we are not, unfortunately, in full communion. This issue does not usually involve any difficulty as far as the lay minister is concerned; if it does, the matter should be referred to the parish priest.

CHAPTER THREE

The Distribution of the Hosts

LET US ASSUME THAT YOU ARE STANDING IN THE PLACE ASSIGNED to you for the distribution of hosts. You will hold the paten (or ciborium) containing the hosts in one hand. As each communicant stands in front of you, take a host from the paten, hold it up to show it to the communicant and say the words 'The Body of Christ'. Take care that you pick up only one host at a time. Some communicants make difficulties if they are given two hosts by mistake, although there is nothing wrong in receiving two hosts.

Catholics in England and Wales were authorised to receive the host on the hand by a decree of the Sacred Congregation for the Sacraments and Divine Worship dated 6 March 1976. This means that the faithful, both adults and children, have a free choice of receiving in the hand or on the tongue. This choice should be respected, whatever the minister's own preference may be. Reception in the hand seems to have been common in the early centuries. The change to reception in the mouth began in the late 8th century.

If the communicant desires to receive on the hand, he will indicate this to you by holding out his hands, the left hand over the right. The minister places a host on the hollowed palm of the left hand. The communicant says 'Amen' and carefully takes the host with the right hand and consumes it. One advantage of this method is that the minister does not have to wait for the 'Amen' before giving the host. On the other hand, you must make sure that the communicant does actually consume the host and does not attempt to walk away with the host in his hand. This only rarely happens, but you should be aware that a communicant might, out of forgetfulness, ignorance, or some wrong motive, do this.

If the communicant wishes to receive on the tongue, he will not, of course, hold out his hand, but instead, after saying 'Amen', he will open the mouth, extend the tongue, and tilt the head back a little. Or at least that was what I was trained to do about half a century ago! Some communicants will be less co-operative than you would wish, unfortunately, and you may find yourself presented with only a tiny tip of the tongue or a narrow slit of mouth. This makes it a little harder for the minister and you have to make certain that the host actually enters the mouth and is not dropped. An important point about administration on the tongue is to wait until the communicant has said 'Amen' before moving your hand forward to give the host.

The 'Amen' said by the communicant when shown the host or the chalice is not simply a formality. It is a declaration of faith that it is truly the Body and Blood of Christ which is being given under the appearance of bread and wine. It is also a sign of the person's desire and intention to receive the sacrament. So this single word has great significance.

There are a few practical points which need to be mentioned. What should you do it a host is dropped? The answer is, quite simply, to pick up the host calmly and with dignity. If it has dropped from the communicant's hand or mouth, then he should consume it. If you yourself drop a host, pick it up and place it to one side of the paten. You can then consume it yourself unobtrusively when you go back to the altar. Fortunately dropping a host does not happen very often.

Another point to note is that some types of host are more fragile and tend to produce crumbs and small fragments. Keep these fragments on the paten and dispose of them as part of the cleansing procedure.

What should be done if you run out of hosts? If you notice in advance that you will need just one or two more, you can break some hosts to provide enough portions. Alternatively you can take a few hosts from the priest (or another hosts minister) standing near you. Otherwise, you will need to take some hosts from the ciborium containing reserved hosts.

To do this, return to the altar and place your paten on the corporal. Fetch the ciborium from the tabernacle, open it on the corporal and transfer some hosts from it to your paten. Leave the ciborium uncovered on the altar and resume the distribution of hosts.

Priests and ministers should remain in their positions until they are no more communicants waiting to receive either hosts or chalice, and then proceed as described in the general routine for ministers in the previous chapter.

Note. It is preferable, and easier, for hosts to be distributed from a paten, which is shaped like a small dish. A church should possess a pair of matching patens for this purpose, and the hosts will be consecrated on them during the Mass. You may, however, have to distribute hosts from a ciborium, which is shaped rather like a chalice and has a lid. It can be awkward having to use a ciborium, especially a small one, when there are many communicants: this is something which should be practised during your training.

CHAPTER FOUR

The Distribution
of the Chalice

LET US ASSUME THAT YOU ARE IN POSITION READY TO ADMINISTER the chalice. It is best to hold the stem of the chalice in your left hand. In your right hand you will be holding the purificator, and when this hand is not otherwise engaged it supports the chalice.

When a communicant approaches, you say 'The Blood of Christ' to which the reply is 'Amen'. You then offer the chalice with both hands and the communicant should take it from you with both hands. This is the safest method of receiving the chalice and the most dignified. It also enables the communicant to see the level of the consecrated wine, which is important: if the minister retains hold the chalice, it is difficult to judge when the communicant has consumed an appropriate amount.

However, if a communicant is unable to hold the chalice properly, or does not hold it securely, then the minister should retain hold of it. Experience shows that younger children are quite capable of taking the chalice into their hands: if they have been properly instructed, they are quite reliable and responsible in this regard. But the minister can still retain hold of the stem if he suspects that the child is not going to hold the chalice securely.

After the communicant has drunk from the chalice, he hands it back to the minister, who then wipes it carefully on the outside and a little way on the inside. This is for the sake of hygiene. The minister should turn the chalice slightly when offering it to the next communicant so that he drinks from a different position.

Medical evidence indicates that the chances of catching infection from the chalice are negligible, especially if the procedures just mentioned are observed. But it is important that ministers are seen to take care with these hygienic measures. Some communicants can be deterred from taking the chalice on hygienic and aesthetic grounds.

It is important to hold the purificator in such a way that it does not get out of control or in the way. From time to time move the purificator around so that you are not wiping the chalice with the same section of it all the time. And do not be afraid to unfold the purificator: there is no rule which says that it must stay done up in its immaculate folds!

It is essential that ministers have plenty of training in administering the chalice, which needs more practice than distributing the hosts.

What should be done if some of the consecrated wine is spilt? Fortunately, this rarely happens. If it does, the minister should act in an unflustered and dignified manner. If only a little is spilt, wipe it up with the purificator. If more than a little is spilt, cover it with the purificator for the time being. Later, after Mass, the floor is washed and the water poured into the sacrarium. If a little is spilt on to clothing, it can be wiped with the purificator. Such clothing and the purificators are then washed or cleaned in the normal way. There is no irreverence in this, because the wine which has been absorbed into the material no longer signifies what it did before the accident.

If your chalice becomes empty during the distribution, indicate to communicants that they can go to another chalice minister. If the distribution of communion is nearly finished, wait in your position, keeping the chalice covered with the purificator to indicate that it is empty. Otherwise, leave your position and carry out the cleansing. Then wait until the others have finished the cleansing so that all the ministers can leave the sanctuary together.

Some churches are adopting the practice of consecrating wine in a single chalice and a flagon. This is to preserve the symbolism of the one cup. At the time of communion, additional chalices are brought to the altar and filled from the flagon. If, therefore, your chalice becomes empty, and if there is still some consecrated wine in the flagon, you can refill your chalice and resume the distribution. However, there is some disagreement about the propriety of consecrating wine in a flagon.

CHAPTER FIVE

Communion
for the Sick and Housebound

A MINISTER MAY TAKE HOLY COMMUNION TO SOMEONE WHO IS SICK or housebound. Authority for this is given in the instruction *Immensae Caritatis* (1973). Some parishes are now making considerable use of ministers to take Holy Communion to houses, hospitals and residential institutions for the benefit of persons who are confined (temporarily or long-term) because of illness, infirmity, or old age. This is of great help to priests as it enables these people to receive Holy Communion more frequently.

Before the rite is described, a few preliminary points need to be made. Firstly, visits by lay ministers do not completely replace visits by a priest, because communicants will want to see the priest for confession, and the position should be made clear to the sick or housebound person. Secondly, the communicant will always be consulted beforehand by the parish priest who will explain why he is proposing to send a lay minister with Communion and why the Church has authorised this ministry. The individual's consent must be given to this arrangement. There are a few people who cannot accept the idea of receiving Holy Communion from a lay minister, and their wishes must be respected. Most sick and housebound persons come to welcome the arrangement, especially when they realise that it will enable them to receive Communion more frequently.

Thirdly, ministers must never arrive unexpectedly or without introduction. The visit should always be by prior arrangement.

Fourthly, it is a good plan to accompany another minister on a visit before going out on your own. This will be a useful experience and will reassure you that the procedure is simple and straightforward. You will find that the minister usually receives a warm welcome and that the visit with Holy Communion is greatly appreciated.

The Rite

Holy Communion is taken to the sick or housebound in the form of a host which is carried in a pyx (this will be described later in this chapter). The rite is as follows:

1. **Greeting.** *The minister greets the communicant and others present in a warm and personal way, using these or similar words:*

Peace to this house and to all who live in it.

2. *The minister puts the Sacrament on the table. He kneels or sits. There may be a period of silent prayer or a hymn may be sung.*

3. **Penitential rite.** *The minister invites the communicant (and all present) to an act of repentance, using these or similar words:*

My brothers and sisters, to prepare ourselves for this celebration, let us call to mind our sins.

After a few moments of silent reflection, all present join in saying 'I confess . . . ' *as at Mass. The minister concludes:*

May almighty God have mercy on us, forgive us our sins, and bring us to everlasting life.
Amen.

4. **Short reading of the word of God.** *The minister, or one of those present, now reads a short passage from scripture: e.g. John 6:54-58; John 14:6-7; John 14:23; John 14:27; 1 Corinthians 11:26; 1 John 4:16.*

5. **Lord's Prayer.** *The minister now introduces the Lord's Prayer with these or other suitable words:*

Now let us pray together to the Father in the words given us by our Lord Jesus Christ.

They all say together: 'Our Father . . . "

6. **Communion.** *The minister shows the Host to the sick person and says:*

This is the Lamb of God who takes away the sins of the world. Happy are those who are called to his supper.

The sick person (and others present) say:

Lord, I am not worthy to receive you, but only say the word and I shall be healed.

The minister goes to the sick person and, showing him the Sacrament, says: 'The Body of Christ'. *The communicant replies* 'Amen' *and is given a host.*

7. **Silence.** *A period of silence may now be observed. Meanwhile the minister cleanses the pyx (see below), unless he is going on to another visit.*

8. **Concluding prayer.** *The minister now says the following or another concluding prayer:*

Let us pray. God our Father, almighty and eternal, we confidently call upon you, that the body of Christ which our brother (sister) has received may bring him (her) lasting health in mind and body. We ask this through Christ our Lord.
Amen.

9. **Blessing.** *The minister then invokes the blessing of God, signing himself and saying:*

May the almighty and merciful God bless and protect us, the Father, and the Son, and the Holy Spirit.
Amen.

Notes on the rite

1. This is the form used in normal circumstances. It is not intended to be a rigid form. It can be modified according to circumstances. Holy Water could be used for a blessing at the beginning. Other suitable forms of the Greeting, the Penitential Rite, the introduction to the Lord's Prayer, and the Final Prayer can be used, especially if they are biblical in form; and various alternatives are given in the official rite (see booklist). There could be a brief discussion or comment on the reading. Petitionary prayers (like the Prayer of the Faithful at Mass) may be said after the reading. A hymn could be sung after communion and at the end. The final blessing could be amplified.

2. On the other hand, the minister should avoid overtaxing someone who is weak, or distressed, or in pain. It is better to keep the rite as brief as possible in such cases.

3. This service of Holy Communion should be seen as closely related to the Mass. To some extent it resembles the Mass: after a penitential rite, there is a brief liturgy of the Word before Holy Communion is administered. As in the Mass, the communicant is fed first by the Word of God and then by the Body of Christ.

4. The relationship of this service to the Mass can be enhanced when ministers go to the sick from a Sunday Mass, bearing hosts consecrated at that Mass and bringing greetings and prayers from the People of God gathered at that celebration of the eucharist. The minister can remind the sick person of this, so that he can feel that he was present in spirit at that particular Mass. When this would be appropriate, the gospel of the day (or part of it) can be used as the reading. The parish Newsletter can also be given to the sick person, and perhaps he could be told something about the Mass: e.g. 'Today twenty children made their first communion at Mass: please pray for them'; or 'Today we had the gospel of the Good Shepherd at Mass and Father Brown said this about it . . . '

5. If the ministers go from a particular Mass to visit the sick, this should be done with some solemnity. The pyxes can be prepared during the distribution of Holy Communion (a minister

can be designated on the rota for this purpose). After the period of silence following Communion, the ministers return to the sanctuary and are given their pyxes by the celebrant. He then sends out the ministers using suitable words, such as:

> Go from this celebration of the Eucharist, taking the Body of Christ to our sick and housebound brothers and sisters, together with our prayers and blessings. By sharing with us at this holy table, may they be strengthened by Christ's saving grace.

The congregation then stands while the ministers walk in procession down the church preceded by the processional cross and the acolytes with candles. When they have left the church, the celebrant resumes the Mass with the Prayer after Communion, the Dismissal, and the Blessing.

It is not recommended that the ministers go out in the final procession at the end of Mass, for several reasons. In particular the link with the congregation's reception of communion is lost because other rites have intervened. Even more so, the ministers should not simply go out of the church informally, slipping out by a side door or something like that. Their going out to the sick is a part of the public celebration: they are sent out officially by priest and people on this sacred eucharistic mission.

There is also a practical advantage in leaving formally before the priest says the Prayer after Communion. Ministers who are going out by car will be able to get away before the congregation crowds into the car park

Members of the congregation are usually impressed by this little ceremony. It reminds them of our duty to pray for the sick and to ensure that they receive the Body of Christ. It signifies the unity of God's People, especially the unity of the sick persons with the congregation at the Mass. It is a particularly important way of continuing or extending the eucharist from the celebration in church on Sunday morning into the world outside and into the life of the people after the Mass itself is over.

6. In the communicant's house or by his bed in hospital there

should be a table covered with a cloth and with candles lit. Communicants who receive regular visits in their own homes usually ensure that this is done. But in hospitals and institutions the provision varies, and ministers should continue with the rite even if the cloth and candles have not been provided. Ministers are not required to take these items with them on visits to the sick.

7. The minister usually carries a pyx containing one or more hosts in a bag or purse which also contains a small corporal and a purificator. These two cloths should not be confused. The corporal is made of linen and is usually folded twice in each direction so when unfolded it shows nine squares. It is customary to have a cross embroidered on the middle front square. The corporal, as its name implies, is the special cloth on which the consecrated host is placed. The purificator is usually folded twice only. It is intended for wiping vessels after they have been cleansed. It should therefore be made of absorbent cloth and not starched. It is often marked with embroidered crosses in each corner: this is so that it is not confused with the towel on which the priest wipes his hands after washing them at Mass.

8. The bag containing the pyx often has a cord so that it can be hung round the neck. There is no obligation to carry it this way: it may be carried in the hand or in a lady's handbag. Sometimes the host is placed in the pyx by the priest, but this may be done by a minister. The minister should be familiar with the routine of obtaining a host from the ciborium in the tabernacle and placing it in the pyx. This procedure should be practised, using unconsecrated hosts. The pyx used for taking communion to the sick is shaped like a man's pocket watch. It has a lid, which either lifts off, or is hinged.

9. When the minister is at the sick person's house, he spreads out the corporal on the table, takes the host from the pyx and places it on the corporal. (Alternatively, he can simply open the pyx for the time being.) He then proceeds with the greeting and penitential rite. If possible, have a glass of water available so that the communicant can drink some water after receiving the host if

he wishes. This is important if a communicant has difficulty in swallowing the host. If the communicant has difficulty in swallowing a whole host, the minister should break off a small piece to give the communicant and consume the rest himself.

10. It is permissible for other persons in the household to receive communion with the sick person in certain circumstances. The parish priest will advise you on this matter.

11. When communion has been received, the pyx should be cleansed in a suitable way. It is usually sufficient to remove all crumbs with the finger and consume them. The pyx is then wiped with the purificator. Water may be used to cleanse the pyx, but it is not necessary.Care must be taken to collect up and consume any crumbs left on the corporal. The corporal and the purificator can now be folded up and replaced in the bag together with the pyx.

12. If for some reason there are hosts or fragments of host left unconsumed, the minister himself should consume them. The pyx should normally be brought back to the church empty of consecrated hosts. The minister should know what the arrangements are for returning the pyxes after sick visits: e.g. are they to be left at the priest's house, or returned to the sacristy at a specified time, or brought back to church the next time the minister visits the church?If the sick calls have been made on a Sunday, it is best to return the pyxes the same day, perhaps through the priest's letter box. This is because Monday is the usual day when the chalices and, if necessary, other vessels are thoroughly washed (in hot water with washing up liquid) and all the cloths which have been used over the weekend at Masses and sick calls are washed and ironed.

13. A sick person who cannot receive Holy Communion in the form of bread may receive in the form of wine. In this case the precious Blood is carried in a special vessel (a phial). This is not a frequent occurrence, but a minister could be asked to take communion to someone in this form. If all the precious Blood is not consumed, the minister must consume the rest himself. The vessel is then cleansed in the usual manner of purification, using water.

CHAPTER SIX

The Rite of Viaticum

THE RITE OF VIATICUM IS USED WHEN A SICK PERSON IS DYING. This is not to be confused with the rite of anointing or what is popularly known as the 'last sacraments' or the 'last rites'. Viaticum (a Latin word meaning 'provision for a journey') is the administration of Holy Communion to someone in likelihood of immediate death to strengthen him with grace for his journey into eternity. Ministers are authorised to administer Communion as viaticum in the Rite of Anointing and Pastoral Care of the Sick: Introduction, section 29 (1972; revised English edition 1984), and in the Code of Canon Law (1983), canon 911.2. The form of the rite to be used by lay ministers is prescribed in *Holy Communion and the Worship of the Eucharist outside Mass* (1973). For practical use, the small booklet *Administration of Communion and Viaticum to the Sick by a Special Minister,* published jointly by Collins, Goodliffe Neale, and Veritas (1978) is recommended.

The minister begins with a greeting and then speaks briefly to those present about the purpose of viaticum. Then follows a period of silent prayer, followed by a penitential rite. After that, it is fitting to have a short reading of the word of God, using one of the texts given in *Holy Communion and Worship of the Eucharist outside Mass* or in the *Rite of Anointing and Pastoral Care of the Sick.*

It is desirable that the sick person renews his baptismal profession of faith before receiving viaticum. If this is to be done, the minister gives a brief introduction and then asks the three credal questions given in the rite. If the condition of the sick person permits, prayers for the sick person are now said in the form of a litany, as given in the rite.

Viaticum is then given, preceded by the Lord's Prayer. After communion, the minister cleanses the pyx (and the phial if communion under the form of wine has been given) in the usual manner. A period of silence may be observed. The rite concludes with a prayer, a blessing, and a sign of peace.

CHAPTER SEVEN

Eucharistic Services outside Mass

1. Exposition

Ministers of Communion are authorised in *Holy Communion and the Worship of the Eucharist outside Mass* (1973), section 91, and also in the Code of Canon Law (1983), canon 943, to hold a service of Exposition of the Blessed Sacrament 'in the absence of a priest or deacon or if they are lawfully impeded'. A minister is permitted to open the tabernacle and place the ciborium on the altar or place the host in the monstrance for a period of adoration. A minister is not permitted to give the blessing with the Blessed Sacrament. At the end of the period of adoration, the minister replaces the Blessed Sacrament in the tabernacle.

During the adoration there should be readings of the word of God, hymns, prayers, and sufficient time for silent prayer. A single genuflection is made in the presence of the Blessed Sacrament exposed. If the monstrance is used, four or six candles should be lit, and for exposition of the Blessed Sacrament in the ciborium, at least two candles.

For exposition in the monstrance there will be a special pyx containing a suitable host in the tabernacle. This host is one of larger size, such as the priest often uses for his own communion at Mass. It is held in a sort of clip called a lunula or lunette, which, as its name suggests, is crescent-shaped like the moon. The lunula is removed from the pyx and inserted (usually in a slide) in the monstrance. Sometimes there is an enlarged form of the lunula which encloses the exposition host in a glass case.

Ministers are advised to read *Holy Communion and the Worship of the Eucharist outside Mass,* sections 82-92, on this subject. A small book published by the CTS, *The Worship of the Eucharist,* contains useful material for services of worship of the Blessed Sacrament.

2. Distribution of Communion outside Mass

Ministers may also, when there is a need, distribute Holy Communion to the faithful outside Mass. This faculty may be used when there is no priest or deacon available; when the priests or deacons are prevented from administering Holy Communion because of another pastoral ministry or because of ill health or advanced age; when the number of the faithful requesting Holy Communion is such that the distribution of Holy Communion outside Mass would be unduly prolonged. The parish priest will show you a copy of the rite to be used when Holy Communion is distributed in church outside Mass: it is contained in the rite *Holy Communion and the Worship of the Eucharist outside Mass* (1973), which also authorised ministers to distribute Communion outside Mass. Authorisation is also given in the Instruction *Immensae Caritatis* (1973) and in the new Code of Canon Law (1983), canons 230.3, 910.2, and 918.

3. Eucharistic services

There are other circumstances in which a minister may be called upon to distribute Holy Communion in the church outside Mass. In some places the shortage of priests causes difficulties. Some churches or chapels may have only occasional visits from a priest. Sometimes a priest going on holiday or having to leave his parish for a time is not able to obtain the services of a supply priest. In such cases, a liturgical service, though not, of course, the Mass itself, can be conducted by a minister, either on a sunday or a weekday. This is authorised in canon 230.3 of the new Code of Canon Law.

Chapter Two: General Routines for Ministers

1. Ministers standing at the ends of the altar before receiving Communion

2. Celebrant and ministers in position for the distribution of communion under both kinds

3. The Ciborium enclosed in veil

4. The Ciborium with veil and lid removed

5. Credence table at the beginning of Mas. Note the four chalice, two patens with hosts, flagons of wine and water, water jug and bowl, towels, corporal, pall, and large host.

6. The vessels with bread and wine arranged on the altar for the Liturgy of the Eucharist. Note the four chalices, two patens with hosts, and large host (which may be broken into many pieces)

7. The Tabernacle. Note the key placed where it can easily be found, and the finger bowl with lid and towel. This modern tabernacle is not covered with veil (conopaeum) or curtains.

(above) Chapter Three: The Distribution of the Hosts
8 (left) on the tongue
9 (right) on the hand

(below) Chapter Four: Communion from the Chalice

0. Offering the chalice	11. Passing the chalice	12. Drinking from the chalice

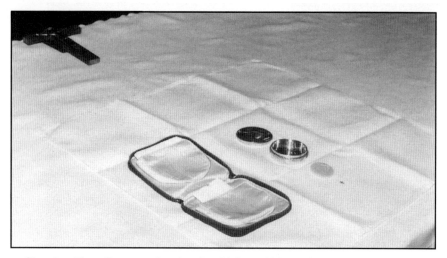

Chapter Five: Communion for the Sick and Housebound
13. The pyx, with lid removed and host to be placed in the pyx. Below, bag in which the pyx is carried, opened to show two pockets; a small corporal in top pocked and a purificator in bottom pocket. The pyx is placed in one of these pockets.

Chapter Seven: Eucharistic Services outside the Mass
14. Monstrance (rear view), with door open to receive host; lunette (or lunula) holding host for exposition; pyx, with door opened, for the reservation of the exposition host in lunette in tabernacle. The pyx is often covered with a 'pocket' shaped veil when in the tabernacle

Such a service is more than simply a distribution of Holy Communion as described in section 2 above. It is a eucharistic celebration and is particularly suitable for Sundays and some weekdays when Mass cannot be celebrated. Here the minister is now able to perform a valuable function in the local Christian community. He can organise, preferably in conjunction with readers and musicians, a service of prayers, ministry of the word, and the distribution of Communion. In this way God's people are not deprived of the Word or of the Body of Christ in Holy Communion.

Services of this sort are already being held, out of necessity, in parts of our own country. They may become more frequent in future, and it is important for the minister to realise the possibility that he might one day be asked to take such a service. Needless to say, you would not be asked to do this without due preparation and briefing.

When Holy Communion is given in church outside Mass, it is, of course, in the form of consecrated hosts which are reserved in the tabernacle.

4. Exposition and Holy Communion

In some churches ministers are holding a service of exposition at the end of which Communion is distributed to those who wish to receive it. This arrangement seems to be popular with congregations and there is much to be said in favour of it. However, some liturgists would disagree with this combination of rites on the grounds that it confuses the emphasis of exposition, namely worship, with that of reception, which is a sacramental rite.

5. Sunday lay-led liturgical celebrations

In an increasing number of places in other countries a shortage of priests means that in some parishes it is not possible to have a Mass every Sunday. This situation is beginning to occur in our own country and will doubtless increase. When a priest is not available, permission is given for a liturgical celebration to be led by a lay person. The Congregation for Divine Worship has now issued some important guidelines for such lay-led liturgies in the *Directory on Sunday Celebrations in the absence of a Priest* (2 June 1988). These celebrations do not have to be a Communion service, and in fact the Directory gives first place to a celebration of the Word of God. However, it seems likely that the laity will prefer these services to include the reception of holy communion. Some Ministers of Holy Communion will probably be invited to lead these Sunday celebrations, or at least to participate in them.

It is beyond the scope of this book to deal with this subject, but Ministers are advised to read the Directory. A book containing resource material and detailed guidelines on lay-led celebrations is in preparation by the Liturgy Office; it is expected to be published shortly by the Bishops' Conference for use in England and Wales.

It is recommended that, unless there is an urgent need to do so, the duties dealt with in this chapter are not covered during the initial training of ministers, but during later in-service training. It will be sufficient during initial training to tell ministers that they are authorised to carry out other duties apart from distributing holy communion.

CHAPTER EIGHT

Some General Points

THIS CHAPTER IS CONCERNED WITH SOME GENERAL POINTS concerning the organisation of ministers and the introduction of Holy Communion under both kinds. As such it is chiefly intended for the guidance of priests, sacristans, servers and those who train ministers. However, ministers need to have some awareness of these points.

1. **Routines in church.** When ministers are to be introduced and even more so when the chalice is to be made available to the people, it is essential to have a clear and straightforward plan for the movements of the people and the positioning of the ministers.

2. **Vessels.** Older chalices are usually unsuitable for the administration of the consecrated wine to large numbers of people. It can also be unsightly to use a mixture of chalices of different sizes and shape. There should be a set of (say) four chalices and two patens of matching and uniform design.

The chalices should be fairly broad so that they are not easily knocked over on the altar. They should be large enough to hold sufficient wine without being filled to the top. They should also be easy to hold: that is, the stem should be designed so that the minister can comfortably hold the chalice in one hand, and the general shape of the chalice should allow for it to be handed easily to the communicant and then back to the minister.

The patens should be large enough to hold all the hosts which are likely to be needed. The use of patens for the distribution of the hosts is far more convenient than the use of ciboria.

3. **Other items.** Jugs or flagons for wine will be needed. The church will need a good stock of purificators: a clean one is needed for each chalice at each Mass. Additional cruets, water jugs, basins and towels will probably be needed. If visits by ministers to the sick are planned, sufficient pyxes (with the appropriate bags, corporals and purificators) will be needed. If communion under both kinds is to be introduced, a larger stock of wine will be needed. Experience will show how much wine will need to be consecrated at each Mass: this should be carefully monitored.

4. **Credence table.** It is strongly recommended that the cleansing of vessels should take place in a side chapel or better still in the sacristy. If, however, this has to be done at the credence table, it is essential to ensure that there is sufficient space on the table for this. Also, the existing credence table may not be large enough to hold all that is required for communion under both kinds: chalices, patens filled with hosts, flagons, cruets, etc.

5. **Cleaning.** Once a week, preferably on a Monday, all the vessels should be thoroughly washed, rinsed and dried, and all the cloths and linen should be laundered. Hygiene is an important consideration, not only 'behind the scenes' but also in the way ministers are seen to administer the chalice.

6. **Standing or kneeling?** Standing is now the most usual posture for receiving both hosts and cup. It is also the most convenient for the actual administration, particularly of the cup. It is also dignified and reverential, and is more in keeping with our participation in the eucharistic meal. Some parishioners will regret the abandonment of the kneeling position, and the parish priest must take care to explain fully why the standing position is considered more appropriate.

7. **Catechesis of the people.** The importance of preparing the congregation for the presence of ministers, the introduction of Holy Communion under both kinds, and the new routines involved

cannot be overstressed. Communicants should be asked to take the chalice with both hands when drinking from it, unless they require assistance in holding it.

8. **The organisation of ministers.** Ministers need to be carefully selected and trained. It is better to invite suitable persons individually, and not make general appeals for volunteers. Some brief notes on a training programme are given at the end of this book. Guidance and help should be available to parish priests from their diocesan liturgical commission.

A secretary is needed to draw up rotas, issue notices, and other duties. It is highly desirable that there should be regular meetings of ministers to discuss business, to review procedures, and to have in-service training. The on-going pastoral care and spiritual formation of the ministers is an important responsibility of the parish priest. From time to time, ministers ought to meet for prayer (preferably the Liturgy of the Hours), a reading of the word, and an address. An annual day of recollection should be held if possible.

PART TWO

BACKGROUND STUDIES

CHAPTER NINE

Ministry and Liturgy

THIS IS THE FIRST TOPIC WE SHOULD THINK ABOUT in our background studies. But as Chapter One had a lot to say about ministry, we need only make a few points here.

This ministry is, firstly, an official ministry, and the appropriate Instructions and sections of Canon Law which give it an authorised and official status have been quoted in various places in Part One. Secondly, it is a lay ministry, which means that the ministers are not quasi-clerics: they are appointed to a ministry which is intended to be exercised by lay men and women.

Thirdly, and perhaps this is the most important point, this is a liturgical ministry. In other words, the ministers have a definite role in the carrying out of the Church's liturgy in the celebration of the eucharist.

If you would like to reflect further on the spiritual and liturgical dimensions of this ministry, it is suggested you read the words of St. Paul in Ephesians 4:1-13 and of St. Peter in 1 Peter 4:10-11; the Constitution on the Sacred Liturgy of the Second Vatican Council, section 29; and the General Instruction of the Roman Missal, chap. 3.

Liturgy

Ministers need to have an understanding of the Church's worship, especially the Mass, and of the sacrament of the Holy Eucharist. One can spend a lifetime reflecting on the great mystery of the Eucharist, and still not exhaust its riches. The Mass itself has a definite structure, and this is something which the minister should study. Indeed there is a great need for the laity as a whole to learn more about the Church's liturgy. It is easy to take for granted that there is nothing more to learn about the Mass and the sacraments because we are so familiar with them.

The second Vatican Council ordered a complete revision of the liturgy. It is significant that liturgy was the first subject to be discussed at the Council. Instead of simply making a few minor changes, as had been expected, the Fathers of the Council found themselves discussing the liturgy in depth. Worship, they declared, is the life of the Church. At the centre of the Church's life and mission is the liturgy, especially the Liturgy of the Word and of the Eucharist. Their teaching was set out in one of the finest documents issued by the Council, the *Constitution on the Sacred Liturgy*. It is strongly recommended that ministers read this document.

As a result, all our rites have been carefully revised and reformed to make them more meaningful and effective. The Mass has been simplified so that the important elements stand out in due prominence. Unimportant accretions have been removed. The arrangement of the readings in the new Lectionary is greatly improved, and we now have every opportunity to proclaim and celebrate the word of God. The eucharistic prayer is now said aloud by the priest, so that we can now associate ourselves closely with the great action of the liturgy.

Why do we use the word 'liturgy' at all? Why is the Mass now officially made up of the Liturgy of the Word and the Liturgy of the Eucharist? 'Liturgy' means 'public office' or 'public action'. The Mass, the Daily Office, the sacraments, and the other rites are called 'liturgical' because they constitute the official, public worship of the Church. This does not mean that private, individual prayer is unimportant. But it does mean that the shared official worship of the Church has a pre-eminent position in the life of the Christian community. This is why there is so much emphasis today on participation in the liturgy.

All this is beautifully expressed in the Constitution on the Liturgy: for example, 'Through the liturgy, especially the divine Eucharistic sacrifice, the work of our redemption is exercised. The liturgy is the outstanding means by which the faithful can express in their lives, and manifest to others, the mystery of Christ and the real nature of the true Church.' (2) 'Christ always associates the Church with himself in the truly great work of giving perfect praise to God and making men and women holy... Rightly, then, the liturgy is considered as an exercise of the priestly office of Jesus Christ... From this it follows that every liturgical celebration, because it is an action of Christ the priest and of his Body the Church, is a sacred action surpassing all others.' (7)

A living liturgy

We are all part of the liturgy. It's our liturgy. It is not a matter of looking on while the priest, the servers and the choir carry out the real actions. We all celebrate and offer up the liturgy together. This is the real meaning of 'participation'.

So our liturgy should be a living liturgy. It should be the celebration today by all of us, together with Christ our High Priest and with the ordained priest, of worship offered day by day to the Father. Every parish should endeavour to develop its liturgy so that it is truly alive.

We come to understand the liturgy by experiencing it, by living it, by doing it. Studying the development and structure of the Mass is important, but it is not enough. In the renewal and revitalisation of the liturgy of a parish, the ministers of communion can play an important part. Their contribution to the eucharistic liturgy, enabling the people more easily to receive Holy Communion, especially under both kinds, will foster within the parish community a greater love and understanding of the Mass.

CHAPTER TEN

The Liturgy of the Word

THE MASS CONSISTS OF TWO LITURGIES: the Liturgy of the Word and the Liturgy of the Eucharist. Before the first of these, there are the Initial Rites, and after the second there are the Concluding Rites.

The two liturgies are closely linked together so as to form one act of worship. We may occasionally have a liturgy of the word on its own, especially when a priest is not available to celebrate Mass. But the Liturgy of the Eucharist is always preceded by the Liturgy of the Word.

The General Instruction of the Roman Missal (=GI) is a very comprehensive account of the Mass in all its aspects. It is written in an attractive and simple style, and ministers are strongly recommended to read it. On the relationship between the two liturgies, the Instruction tells us: 'The table of God's word and of Christ's body is prepared and from it the faithful are instructed and nourished." (GI 8)

The Initial Rites

These rites 'have the character of beginning, introduction, and preparation. The purpose of these rites is to make the assembled people a unified community and to prepare them properly to listen to God's word and celebrate the eucharist.'(GI 24)

After the optional entry or opening hymn (or chant), the priest begins with 'In the name of the Father . . . ', because everything we do as Christians is done in the name of the Trinity and in relationship to the Trinity.

The greeting is an important action and is one of the oldest elements in the Mass. It sets the atmosphere of mutual love in Jesus Christ which should characterise the local Church as it gathers to celebrate the Word and the Eucharist.

The most important part of the Initial Rites is the Prayer (or Collect). This prayer gathers together the individual prayers of the faithful into one public prayer, pronounced by the President in our name. The prayer often sums up the theme of the celebration, especially on feast days. Notice the Trinitarian pattern of the prayer: it is addressed to God the Father, through the Son, and in the Holy Spirit. This pattern runs throughout the Mass. The eucharistic sacrifice is offered to the Father, by and through the Son, and in the Holy Spirit.

The Liturgy of the Word

'In the readings, explained by the homily, God speaks to his
people of redemption and salvation and nourishes their spirit;
Christ is present among the faithful through his word. Through
the chants the people make God's word their own . . . ' (GI 33)

This part of the Mass is not simply an opportunity to learn about the Word, although we continue to develop our understanding of it throughout our lives. We refer to it as a liturgy because it is a public action of the Christian community. The action is that of proclaiming God's living word and the salvation won for us by Christ.

God's word is basic to our lives as Christians, as it was to the Jews. It is from the Jewish synagogue service held on the sabbath for readings and prayer that our Liturgy of the Word has developed. A vivid description of this service is found in Luke 44:16-21. Jesus and his disciples regularly went to it, and the early Jewish converts to Christianity continued to attend the synagogue. When they were no longer able to go to the synagogue, they held a similar service of their own. In time it became a regular practice to celebrate the eucharist after a service of readings, and so the pattern of the Mass as we know it evolved.

God's word makes great demands on us: we have to accept it and respond to it. At the Liturgy of the Word, the people make their response to the word of God in the 'responsorial psalm' and the 'gospel acclamation', and these parts of the liturgy are very important.

In the readings and the homily, the people are nourished at the table of the word of the Lord. On Sundays and solemnities 'they express their adherence to it through the profession of faith" and 'moved by this word, they pray in the general intercessions for the needs of the Church and for the world's salvation' (GI 33)

There are many inspiring references in the scriptures to the power of God's word, including Hebrews 4:12-13; 1 Peter 1:24-25; 1 Thess. 2:13; 2 Thess. 3:1; Ephes. 6:17; Col. 1:4-6; and James 1:19-25. These passages will help us to reflect on the central importance of the word in our lives. As St. Paul wrote, 'Christ's message, in all its richness, must live in your hearts'. (Col. 3:16)

CHAPTER ELEVEN

The Liturgy of the Eucharist

THIS CONSISTS OF THREE SECTIONS:

The Preparation of the Gifts
The Eucharistic Prayer
The Rite of Communion.

The Preparation of the Gifts

The celebrant now moves from the Presidential chair to the altar, and takes the gifts of bread and wine which are later to be consecrated. This part of the Mass, which is essentially practical, was originally carried out in silence and without any prayers.

The Eucharistic Prayer

This part of the Mass is not simply a series of prayers. We call it a liturgy because it is a public action of the whole Christian community. What does this action consist of? It is, in fact, a three-fold action:

(1) REMEMBRANCE

In the first place, it is an action of 'making a remembrance' of Christ's death and resurrection. He told us 'Do this in remembrance of me'. Faithful to Christ's command, we celebrate the eucharist because this is the memorial of himself which he left us.

We do not simply recall his death and resurrection as past events. Through the eucharist they are a continuing reality in the present for us.

(2) THANKSGIVING

In the second place, it is an action of 'giving thanks', which is the meaning of the word 'eucharist'. When Jesus said 'Do this . . . ', what exactly was the 'this' that he was referring to? He had just celebrated a special meal with his disciples. At this he carried out the customary Jewish meal rituals. In particular there was the blessing of God associated with the taking of bread before the main part of the meal, and there was also a very solemn blessing of God associated with the third cup of wine after the main meal had been eaten.

To the Jews, 'blessing God' means giving thanks and praise to God for something. In this sense, God was 'blessed' at the taking of the bread for 'bringing forth bread from the earth'. After the meal, he was 'blessed' for giving nourishment to all men, for giving the Jews the promised land, and for Jerusalem.

Jesus pronounced these blessings in accordance with Jewish custom at the Last Supper. But, as we know, he transformed these blessings. The bread and wine, taken up as gifts from God, became the Body and Blood of Christ, given for us. He gave them to his disciples and told them to do this action in remembrance of him.

Today we use the word 'consecration' to describe the action whereby the gifts of bread and wine become the Body and Blood of Christ. This action is, however, still the pronouncing of blessing or thanksgiving over the gifts of bread and wine. The Jews gave thanks for their deliverance from bondage in Egypt and for all God's goodness to them. Christians give thanks for their deliverance from the bondage of death and sin. So every celebration of the eucharist is a thanksgiving for the death and resurrection of Jesus Christ, which has brought about our salvation.

(3) OFFERING

In the third place, it is a sacrificial offering. We offer to the Father the sacrifice of Christ on the Cross. This sacrifice cannot be repeated, but it is continually recalled, made a present reality, re-enacted and offered to the Father. The Mass is a sacrifice of praise and thanksgiving, and a sacrifice of expiation for the sins of the living and the dead.

At the sacrifice of the Mass, Christ is both priest and victim. As our High Priest he offers his sacrifice of himself to the Father. The priest of the Church is ordained to represent the Church. He presides at the eucharistic celebration, speaking in the name of the Church and of Christ himself.

The structure of the Eucharistic Prayer

The eucharistic prayer must not be seen as a collection of prayers which are largely the concern of the priest; nor must they be seen as a formality surrounding the central moment of consecration. The eucharistic prayer consists of the liturgical action already described, an action of remembrance, thanksgiving and offering. Although the transformation of the bread and wine takes place at the moment of consecration, the whole of the eucharistic prayer is consecratory. The priest is never allowed to consecrate bread and wine except as part of the whole eucharistic action.

The eucharistic prayer is pronounced by the priest in our name: he prays in the plural. The congregation should not, therefore, engage in completely separate, parallel devotions of their own during the eucharistic prayer. They should be closely associated with the celebrant as he pronounces the prayer, and give their assent to it in the appropriate places.

It is significant that the people begin and end the eucharistic prayer: they respond to the call to give thanks in the opening dialogue and they conclude the eucharistic prayer with the great Amen. In addition they make important acclamations at the 'Holy, holy... ' and after the consecration.

The pattern of the Eucharistic Prayer is a sequence of four actions:

(1) *THANKSGIVING*

After the opening dialogue, the priest proclaims the first set of thanksgiving statements (the preface) and this is followed by the acclamation 'Holy, holy'. He then resumes the thanksgiving.

(2) *INSTITUTION NARRATIVE*

The priest calls down the Holy Spirit to transform the gifts of bread and wine, and then proceeds to the consecration first of the bread and then of the wine, using the narrative of the institution at the Last Supper. The people then proclaim the mystery of faith: there are four forms from which to choose, and each expresses very strikingly and succinctly the great paschal mystery being celebrated in the eucharist.

(3) *REMEMBRANCE AND OFFERING*

The priest makes a specific remembrance of Christ's death, resurrection and ascension, and then goes on to offer up the sanctified gifts, which sacramentally represent Christ's sacrifice, to the Father. He now calls on the Holy Spirit once more, this time asking that we might receive the fruits of Holy Communion.

(4) *INTERCESSIONS*

This is an appropriate moment to make intercessions. These are general intercessions for the whole Church, not the specific intercessions of the Prayer of the Faithful. The celebrant prays for the Church, the Pope, the bishop, and all God's people living and dead. Then comes the final doxology and the great Amen in which the whole people signify their assent to the eucharistic prayer.

The Rite of Communion

After various preliminaries, priest and people receive the Body and Blood of Christ in Holy Communion. This is the completion of Christ's command 'Take this and eat/drink'. This reception is the culmination of our participation in the eucharistic liturgy. Our participation in it is less than complete if we do not receive.

The Concluding Rites

These consist quite simply of a prayer that we might obtain the fruits of the eucharistic action, the blessing, and the dismissal.

Notes

It is suggested that you take the text of Eucharistic Prayers 2, 3 and 4, and trace the sequence of the various sections using the schema given above. It should be noted that Eucharistic Prayer 1 (the traditional Roman Canon) follows a slightly different pattern.

The following New Testament passages are of great importance: the accounts of the Last Supper in Matthew 26, Mark 14, and Luke 22; the teaching of Our Lord about the bread of life in John 6; the teaching of Paul about the eucharist in 1 Cor. 10 and 11; and the description in Hebrews 9 of how the new covenant has been sealed by the blood of Christ. Much of the Letter to the Hebrews is devoted to the sacrifice and priesthood of Christ.

CHAPTER TWELVE

The Sacrament of the Holy Eucharist

The sacramental Church

So far, we have been discussing the eucharist as the liturgical action in which we make remembrance of and give thanks for the death and resurrection of Jesus Christ, and offer up once more to the Father the sacrifice which Christ made of himself on the cross. Our own celebration of the eucharistic liturgy is made complete by receiving Holy Communion.

When we receive Holy Communion, we are receiving one of the sacraments of the Church, and in this chapter we shall be looking at the sacramental aspects of the Holy Eucharist.

By becoming man and living among us, Jesus Christ has given a dignity to our world. By using ordinary things such as bread and wine as his sacred signs, he has transformed and sanctified our material world. So we can see the world, under Christ, as sacramental. Christ himself in his humanity is a sacrament (cf. Col. 1:15-20), and so is his Church (cf. second Vatican Council, Dogmatic Constitution on the Church, 1).

The Church founded by Jesus Christ is a sacramental Church: its whole life is based on the sacraments. God has ordained that the saving merits of Jesus Christ's death and resurrection come to us through the Church and through the sacraments of the Church.

There is a traditional definition of a sacrament in the Catechism Q. 249: 'A sacrament is an outward sign of inward grace, ordained by Jesus Christ, by which grace is given to our souls'. Fr. Herbert McCabe OP has given a more comprehensive definition in his useful book The Teaching of the Catholic Church: A New Catechism of Christian Doctrine (CTS 1985) (Q. 68):

> A sacrament is a sacred sign by which we worship
> God, his love is revealed to us and his saving
> work accomplished in us. In the sacraments God
> shows us what he does and does what he shows us.

The sacrament of the Holy Eucharist

We receive grace through the sacraments of the Church, beginning with baptism. After baptism, the Holy Eucharist is pre-eminent among the seven sacraments of the Church. It is the sacrament in which Christ, under the forms of bread and wine, is truly present, with his Body and Blood, in order to offer himself in an unbloody manner to the Father, and to give himself to the faithful as nourishment for their souls.

The Eucharist is a sacred meal. This meal both symbolises the unity of the Church in love and brings about this unity. It recalls to our minds and hearts the sacrifice of Christ, and is a pledge of the future unity of mankind in the Kingdom of God.

The outward sign of the Eucharist consists of bread and wine as the 'matter' and the words of institution as the 'form'. All the sacraments confer sanctifying grace on the soul. In addition, each sacrament confers a specific grace of its own.

The chief fruit of the Eucharist is an intrinsic union with Christ.Secondly, the Eucharist, as food and nourishment of the soul, preserves and increases the supernatural life of the soul. Finally, the Eucharist is a pledge of heavenly bliss and of the future resurrection of the body.

The sacraments are necessary for the salvation of mankind because they are the means appointed by God for the attainment of salvation. The reception of the Eucharist is especially important, as Christ himself said:

I tell you most solemnly, if you do not eat the
flesh of the Son of Man and drink his blood, you
will not have life in you. Anyone who eats my flesh
and drinks my blood has eternal life, and I shall
raise him up on the last day.   (John 6:54)

The purpose of the Eucharist is the nourishment of the soul:
without it, supernatural life cannot be permanently maintained.

CHAPTER THIRTEEN

Holy Communion
under Both Kinds

The Chalice restored

ONE OF THE REASONS WHY LAY MINISTERS ARE NEEDED is because
we are now able to receive Holy Communion under both kinds.
Permission to receive the chalice at Mass on Sundays was granted
to the Catholics of England and Wales by the Holy See on 8 May
1985. Permission had previously been given for reception of the
chalice at weekday Masses.

After many centuries, lay people are now allowed once more to
receive the chalice at Mass. This should be a cause of much happi-
ness because it means that Holy Communion can be received under both the sacramental species. It is to be hoped that priests who
have not yet introduced the chalice will do so, and that the faithful
will welcome this opportunity to receive under both kinds.

Ministers of Communion can, of course, administer either the
hosts or the chalice at Mass. They are not permitted to give Communion under both kinds by intinction: only a priest or deacon
can do this. The Holy See laid down certain conditions. The laity
must be properly instructed and prepared for receiving the chalice.
They must be reminded of the teaching of the Church (as set out
by the Council of Trent) that the whole Christ and the entire
sacrament is received when communion is taken in one kind only.
They must be free to make a personal choice whether to receive
the chalice or not. Finally, the chalice is not to be administered at
large outdoor Masses or at Masses attended by large numbers of

the faithful who have not received instruction on Communion under both kinds.

Christ's institution

It is important for ministers to understand the significance of communion under both kinds. Christ gave us the Eucharist in the form of both eating and drinking. It is natural to have both eating and drinking at a meal, and this was the case at the Last Supper. In fact, drinking wine at a festive meal had very great significance for the Jews:

Jesus took some bread, and when he had said the blessing, he broke it and gave it to the disciples. 'TAKE IT AND EAT', he said, this is my body.

Then he took a cup, and when he had returned he gave it to them. 'DRINK ALL OF YOU FROM THIS', he said, 'for this is my blood, the blood of the covenant, which is to be poured out for many' *(Mt 26:26-28)*

By receiving Communion under both kinds, we are obeying Christ's command at the Last Supper more fully, and we are celebrating the Eucharist more nearly as he instituted it. Communion under both kinds brings out the full meaning and richness of the sacramental sign.

Jesus had previously told the Jews: 'I tell you most solemnly, if you do not eat the flesh of the Son of Man AND DRINK HIS BLOOD, you will not have life in you'. *(John 6:53)*

The importance of signs

Jesus made great use of signs in his teaching and also in his institution of the Eucharist. To understand the sacraments and to celebrate them meaningfully we need to be open to the language of signs. Jesus used simple, familiar, everyday things to bring out his meaning. For the Eucharist he chose the basic ingredients of a meal: bread and wine.

These were simple and also very powerful and rich signs. Eating and drinking are basic activities in our lives. The Jews saw eating as creative because it maintained the human life created by God. A meal signified not only nourishment but fellowship and unity. To Christians the eucharistic meal is a symbol of the heavenly banquet.

Bread is a basic food. It symbolised life to the Jews and reminded them of the life-giving manna. Jesus enriched this understanding of the significance of bread, the bread of life: it became his flesh given for the life of the world.

To the Jews wine had an even greater and richer significance. It was not only an everyday drink, but it also in different contexts symbolised healing, joy, and love. It also symbolised blood and sacrifice. To receive Christ under both forms is to respond more fully to these two signs as instituted by Christ himself.

Why is the chalice now offered to the laity?

In the early centuries of the Church's history, the laity received under both kinds. As the Church spread through Europe, many of the new Christians were uninstructed, and from about the 5th century lay people began to receive communion less frequently. There were several reasons for this. Worship in church had become more formalised and clericalised, the people became more like spectators than participants at Mass. The popular understanding of the Mass became somewhat distorted. More attention was given to worshipping Christ at the elevation than to receiving him in communion.

Combined with these factors there was a growth in scrupulosity together with an excessive preoccupation with sinfulness and unworthiness. There was even more dropping away from receiving the chalice than receiving the host. It is probably nearer the truth to say that the laity withdrew itself from the chalice than to say that the Church withdrew the chalice from the laity.

At the Reformation in the 16th century the reformers made

much of restoring the chalice to the laity. The Council of Trent discussed the issue and decided it would not be opportune to restore the chalice to the laity. The Council confirmed the teaching of the Church that in receiving under either kind one receives the whole Christ, body and blood, soul and divinity, and one receives the whole sacrament.

In our own day, the reasons which led the Council of Trent to take a cautious view about restoring the chalice no longer apply. There is more openness on such issues and a powerful spirit of liturgical renewal. The second Vatican Council opened the way to restoring the chalice (see section 55 of the Constitution on the Sacred Liturgy). This movement was developed still further in the General Instruction of the Roman Missal, especially in section 240:

> The sign of communion is more complete when given under both kinds, since in that form the sign of the eucharistic meal appears more clearly. The intention of Christ that the new and eternal covenant be ratified in his blood is better expressed, as is the relation of the eucharistic banquet to the heavenly banquet.

The Church actually encourages us to receive under both kinds:

> The faithful should be urged to take part in the rite which brings out the sign of the eucharistic meal more fully. (GI 241)

This, surely, is a matter in which we should follow the explicit teaching of the Church and welcome the opportunity to receive the chalice, as the priest does, at Mass.

APPENDIX

Documents and Texts

Second Vatican Council: *Constitution on the Sacred Liturgy* (Sacrosanctum Concilium) (December 4th, 1963)

General Instruction of the Roman Missal (March 26th, 1970)

Congregation for the Discipline of the Sacraments, instruction, *Immensae Caritatis* (January 29th, 1973)

Holy Communion and the Worship of the Eucharist outside Mass (Eucharistiae Sacramentum) (June 21st, 1973)

Administration of Communion and Viaticum to the Sick by a special minister (taken from the previous document, gives the rites to be used) published jointly by Collins, Goodliffe Neale, and Veritas. (1978)

The Worship of the Eucharist (C.T.S.)

The Pastoral Care of the Sick (Geoffrey Chapman, revised edition, 1984)

Code of Canon Law (1983) (canons 230, 910, 911, 943)

Congregation for Divine Worship: *Directory on Sunday Celebrations in the absence of a Priest* (June 22nd 1988)

Further Reading

The Catechism of the Catholic Church (1994), Part Two: The Celebration of the Christian Mystery. Sections 1066-1209 deal with liturgy in general, 1322-1419 with the Eucharist.

Donald A. Withey, *Catholic Worship: An Introduction to Liturgy* (Kevin Mayhew, 1990), esp. chapters 8-12.

Donald A. Withey, *Why Receive the Chalice?* (Kevin Mayhew, 1990). A brief account of the Mass and the reception of Holy Communion under both kinds.

Stephen Dean (ed). *Celebration: The Liturgy Handbook* (Geoffrey Chapman, 1993) especially Units 1, 2, 3.

Outline of a Training Programme for Ministers of Holy Communion

It is recommended that ministers should receive at least ten hours of initial training. This could be organised over two days (say, two Saturdays, five hours on each day plus an hour for lunch), but my own experience is that a five week course consisting of two hour sessions is preferable. The following is a suggested programme arranged over five sessions. To indicate the timing of each activity, it will be assumed that the meetings take place in the evening (perhaps after evening Mass), starting at 7.30 and conclude at 9.30.

WEEK ONE

7.30   READING: Ephes. 4:1-13. PRAYER.

7.40   TALK AND DISCUSSION: MINISTRY
        Ministry in the Church. The nature and functions of the eucharistic ministry. Spiritual formation.
        Liturgical foundations.

8.30   SKILL TRAINING: Ministers' routines at Mass.
        The vessels and their cleansing.

9.20   PRAYER and blessing.

WEEK TWO

7.30   READING: 1 Cor. 11:23-27. PRAYER.

7.40   TALK AND DISCUSSION: THE EUCHARIST 1
        Understanding the Liturgy of the Eucharist. Its origins and shape.

8.30   SKILL TRAINING: Administering the hosts and chalice.

9.20   PRAYER and blessing.

WEEK THREE

7.30   READING: Hebrews 9:15-28. PRAYER.

7.40   TALK AND DISCUSSION: THE EUCHARIST - 2
The structure of the eucharistic prayers.
Communion as part of the eucharistic action.

8.30   SKILL TRAINING: Administering the hosts and
chalice. (further practice)

9.20   PRAYER and blessing.

WEEK FOUR

7.30   In the church: Practice on the sanctuary.
    (movements, tabernacle, etc.)

8.00   READING: John 6:53-58. PRAYER.

8.10   TALK AND DISCUSSION: COMMUNION UNDER
BOTH KINDS: Its significance. The importance of the
chalice.

8.50   SKILL TRAINING: Taking communion to the sick
and the housebound.

9.20   PRAYER and blessing.

WEEK FIVE

7.30   READING: John 6:32-51 PRAYER.

7.40   TALK AND DISCUSSION: THE SACRAMENT OF
THE HOLY EUCHARIST
Sacramental aspects of Holy Communion.

8.30   SKILL TRAINING: Summary of other ministerial
duties.
Further practice and discussion as needed.

9.20   PRAYER and blessing.

Rite of Commissioning Ministers of Holy Communion

Ministers are commissioned by the bishop of the diocese, or more usually by the parish priest acting on behalf of the bishop. The commissioning should normally be held at a parish Mass on a Sunday or feast day, in the presence of the community to be served by the new ministers. It takes place after the homily.

The priest will usually begin by talking about this ministry, reminding the ministers and the people of the parish of its significance. He then presents to the people those who are to be commissioned, using these or similar words:

Our brothers and sisters N. and N. are to be entrusted with administering the eucharist, with taking communion to the sick, and with giving it as viaticum to the dying.

The priest pauses and then addresses the new ministers:

In this ministry you must be examples of Christian living in faith and conduct; you must strive to grow in holiness through this sacrament of unity and love. Remember that, though many, we are one body because we share the one bread and one cup.

As ministers of holy communion be, therefore, especially observant of the Lord's command to love your neighbour. For when he gave his body as food to his disciples, he said to them: 'This is my commandment, that you should love one another as I have loved you.'

The new ministers then stand before the priest who asks them these questions:

Are you resolved to undertake the office of giving the body and blood of the Lord to your brothers and sisters, and so serve to build up the Church?

℟.   **I am.**

Are you resolved to administer the holy eucharist with the utmost care and reverence?

℟.   **I am.**

All stand. The new ministers kneel and the priest invites the people to pray:

Dear friends in Christ,
let us pray with confidence to the Father;
let us ask him to bestow his blessings on our brothers and sisters,
chosen to be ministers of the eucharist.

Pause for silent prayer. The priest then continues:

Merciful Father
creator and guide of your family,
bless ✠ our brothers and sisters N. and N.
May they faithfully give the bread of life to your people.
Strengthened by this sacrament,
may they come at last to the banquet of heaven.
We ask this through Christ our Lord.

℟.   **Amen.**

At this Mass, it is fitting to include a petition for the new Ministers in the General Intercession and for the new Ministers to carry the vessels with the bread and wine to the altar during the Preparation of the Gifts.

Commissioning outside Mass

If the commissioning is to take place outside Mass, the people of the parish should assemble in the church. An appropriate song is sung and the celebrant greets the people. There normally follows a short Liturgy of the Word. The readings are taken, either in whole or in part, from the liturgy of the day or from the readings for the Institution of Acolytes, Lectionary Vol. III p.336.

The rite then continues as above. Finally the celebrant blesses the people and dismisses them in the usual way. The rite concludes with an appropriate song.

[Adapted from Study Book for Special Ministers of Holy Communion *(CTS 1980), with permission. Ritual text © ICEL 1978.]*

Rite of Renewal of Commitment by Ministers of Communion

Ministers are normally commissioned for a year at a time. They are expected to attend a day of recollection each year. [It is also recommended that ministers meet from time to time for in-service training and on-going liturgical formation, for business meetings to discuss matters concerning their ministry, and for a social gathering.]

They should renew their commitment annually, preferably in the presence of the parish. The solemnity of the Body and Blood of Christ is a very suitable occasion for this.

The following is a suggested rite for renewal of commitment. Other similar wording may be used.

The renewal takes place after the homily. The ministers stand in front of the parish priest, who presides at the renewal on behalf of the bishop.

Priest: Are you resolved to continue to undertake the office of minster of holy communion for the service and growth of the Church?

Ministers: **I am.**

Priest: Are you resolved to continue to administer the holy eucharist with the utmost care and reverence?

Ministers: **I am.**

Priest: Are you resolved to continue to strive more earnestly than ever to live the Christian life, to give good example, and to take your faith more seriously?

Ministers: **I am.**

The ministers then kneel. The priest continues:

Priest: Dear friends in Christ,
let us pray with confidence to the Father;
let us ask him to bestow his blessings on our brothers
and sisters chosen to be ministers of the Eucharist.

Merciful Father, creator and guide of your family,
bless ✠ our brothers and sisters.
May they faithfully give the bread of Life to your
people.
Strengthened by this sacrament
may they come at last to the banquet of heaven.
We ask this through Christ our Lord.

Ministers: **Amen.**

Priest: You are authorised to continue to assist the priests
and people of this parish in the distribution of holy
communion for the next twelve months. During the
year you should attend a day of prayer and, as far as
possible, other meetings arranged for ministers. You
should renew your commitment before the priests
and people of this parish next year at about this time.

[Adapted from Study Book for Special Ministers of Holy Communion
(CTS 1980), pp.17-18, with permission.)